HONOR THY MUSIC®

SONGBIRD'S FLIGHT

COUNTRY MUSIC FOUNDATION PRESS

222 FIFTH AVENUE SOUTH · NASHVILLE, TENNESSEE 37203

978-0-915608-33-1

THIS PUBLICATION WAS CREATED BY THE STAFF OF THE COUNTRY MUSIC HALL OF FAME® AND MUSEUM.

EDITOR: JAY ORR

PRINTER: LITHOGRAPHICS, INC., NASHVILLE, TENNESSEE.

Harris, Coldwater Canyon, California, 1976. *Photo: Michael Dobo / Dobophoto.com*

CONTENTS

Artifact photos by Bob Delevante.

ACKNOWLEDGMENTS

We hope that this book and the exhibition it accompanies convey some measure of Emmylou Harris's indelible contribution to the past, present, and future of country music. The book and exhibition are collaborations between Harris, her representatives, her friends and associates, and the Country Music Hall of Fame and Museum.

Telling Harris's story involves telling the story of the musical community that she has engendered. Many members of that community loaned artifacts, documents, instruments, and photographs, to illustrate the depth and texture of Harris's musical life. We are grateful to those who aided the book and exhibition, including Harris, Maple Byrne, Rodney Crowell, Steve Fishell, Michele Fisher, Bonnie Garner, Manfred Gerspacher, Phil Kaufman, Paul Kennerley, Ken Levitan, Fayssoux Starling McLean, Buddy Miller, Nina Miller, Kevin Spellman, Jon Randall Stewart, and Kathi Whitley.

Photographer Dan Reeder deserves special mention for the use of his many images. Other photographers who contributed include Danny Clinch, Bob Delevante, Michael Dobo, Kim Gottlieb-Walker, Doug Hanners, Chris Hollo/Grand Ole Opry Archives, Les Leverett/Grand Ole Opry Archives, Lawson Little, Steve Lowry/Banner Archives, David McClister, Ron McKeown, Michael Wilson, and Katherine Wilkes Harvill on behalf of her father, Tom Wilkes.

Many museum staff members devoted time and talent to the book and the exhibit. Space prohibits listing them all, but some deserve mention here. Vice President of Museum Services Brenda Colladay and Executive Director of Exhibits John Reed led the curatorial team, which consisted of Peter Cooper, Mick Buck, Shepherd Alligood, Bryan Jones, and Senior Registrar Elek Horvath. Editor Jay Orr, Senior Creative Director Warren Denney, Senior Design Manager Bret Pelizzari, Associate Creative Director Jeff Stamper, and Associate Director of Production Chris Richards deserve special recognition.

Owner's manual for the 1970 Ford Pinto that Harris drove the first time she met Gram Parsons.

DEAR MUSEUM PATRON,

Emmylou Harris has spent a lifetime teaching master classes in integrity, musicality, individuality, and harmony—teaching them by example rather than by admonition.

She seeks, finds, and inspires the best in others, whether in melody and rhyme or in kindness and generosity.

She has surrounded herself with a bounty of songs and collaborators. In telling her story, we find ourselves talking about people she has sung with—Bob Dylan, Dolly Parton, Linda Ronstadt, Bruce Springsteen, and Neil Young come to mind—and about the people whose compositions she has brought to wider attention, including Rodney Crowell, Steve Earle, Kieran Kane, Paul Kennerley, Buddy and Julie Miller, David Olney, Gillian Welch, and Lucinda Williams.

Seeking out the best work of others, Harris has found and recorded devastatingly beautiful songs including Crowell's "'Til I Gain Control Again," Townes Van Zandt's "Pancho and Lefty," and Welch's "Orphan Girl." Her own uncompromising artistry allowed her to write songs that matched their power and impact, including "Boulder to Birmingham," "Prayer in Open D," and "Bang the Drum Slowly," the latter written about her father, who spent nine months as a prisoner of war in Korea.

Emmylou restored the Louvin Brothers to popularity a decade after Ira Louvin's death. She carried forward the concept of "Cosmic American Music," a musical blend—envisioned by her mentor, Gram Parsons—that combined soulful rock energy and deep country roots. She hired Tony Brown, Sam Bush, Rodney Crowell, Steve Fishell, Buddy Miller, Ricky Skaggs, and other notables for her band, elevating and accelerating their grand careers.

She recorded albums that focused listeners' attention on traditional country, on bluegrass, and on music now covered by the broad flannel blanket of Americana.

Her charitable endeavors have comforted endangered children, aided the preservation of country music, and saved the lives of hundreds of animals.

And she's a damn great singer. One for the ages.

Welcome to *Emmylou Harris: Songbird's Flight*. I am proud that our museum is telling this great American story of gently righteous triumph.

Sincerely,

Kyle Young
CEO

A Mystical Reverence

BY RODNEY CROWELL

In my forty-plus years of friendship and collaboration with Emmylou Harris, I have observed, in my own behavior and in that of others, a rather mystical reverence for what is often described as her "angelic presence." It's true, there is something otherworldly in Emmylou's persona that inspires devotion among friends and fans alike. And yet, it would be misleading to suggest that she isn't deeply grounded in the here and now. The Emmylou I know is passionately committed to family, truth, humor, generosity, integrity, equality, friendship, conviction, loyalty, purpose, music, storytelling, befriending ex-husbands, baseball, and dogs. Emmylou is the beautiful valedictorian

From left: Rodney Crowell, Emmylou Harris, and Emory Gordy Jr. 1976.
Photo: Dan Reeder

girl-next-door who, in the late sixties, followed her folksinger's dream to New York City and, with subsequent stints in Washington, Los Angeles, and Nashville, became a world-renowned recording artist, who, to this day, bears up under a touring schedule that would break a coal miner's back.

When I'm asked to describe what it is about Emmylou that is so beloved by her fans, without hesitation I point out that like Willie Nelson, Johnny Cash, Loretta Lynn, John Prine, and Kris Kristofferson, she has the poet's soul. It is the nature of these artists' souls that has held our interest for a half-century or more. Although Emmylou is not necessarily known as a songwriter, her songs—"Red Dirt Girl," "Michelangelo," and "Tulsa Queen," to name but three— are at the top of my list of favorite Emmylou Harris recordings. It is my heartfelt belief that Emmylou's long-standing artistic relevance is to be found in the very essence of who she is—a goddess in blue jeans with the voice of an angel.

RODNEY CROWELL

Left: Crowell and Harris, 2012.
Photo: David McClister

Below: Crowell and Harris,
c. 1975. *Photo: Dan Reeder*

Opposite page: Harris, c. 1975.
Photo: Dan Reeder

Mangle With Care

BY PHIL KAUFMAN

Ask me who my second favorite person is.

No, don't. It doesn't matter. My favorite is Emmylou Harris, and that's not going to change. I've worked with Mick Jagger, Joe Cocker, Etta James, Rosanne Cash, Nanci Griffith, Frank Zappa, and a whole bunch of others. But there's no one like Emmylou.

I met her at the Chateau Marmont hotel in Hollywood. I was working with Gram Parsons, who had hired Emmylou to sing with him on his first album. She was very shy, and I remember she was knitting while Gram was recording. Then she came in to sing, and I became infected with the "Wow" syndrome. She starts singing, and it's "Wow." Gram wanted her to be Tammy Wynette to his George Jones, and she was all that and more.

People call me the Road Mangler. I'm a road manager, which means I take care of people. I keep them out of harm's way. I took the most and best care of Emmylou, because, as I said, she's my favorite. After Emmy wowed everyone on Gram's two solo records, Gram gave up his George Jones aspirations by dying young. I took care of Gram by fulfilling a promise I made to him, which was to cremate his body in the California desert. Not

From left: Harris's daughter Meghann Ahern, Harris, and Phil Kaufman backstage at New York's Central Park Summer Concert Series, 1980.
Photo: Lawson Little

9 Music Square South #339
Nashville, Tennessee 37203

PHIL KAUFMAN
Road Mangler Deluxe

Height: 5'7"   Weight: 179 lbs + tax   Birthdate: 4-26-?
Hometown: Where The Bus Is Parked

EMAIL: PHKAUF@AOL.COM

Phil's nickname is "Mangler". Phil moves people, not equipment. Phil is also the world's premier Road Mangler. Honest! Phil is also a PADI Divemaster. Phil is the author of "Road Mangler Deluxe".

Hobbies: Trashing Hotel Rooms
         Mooning

Printed in the USA by Americans

Above: Kaufman's business card, with a 1967 photo as an inmate at FCI Terminal Island, a federal prison in California.

Opposite page: Kaufman and Harris outside New York's Beacon Theatre, December 1993.

everyone agreed with what I did, but Emmylou never broached the subject. She hired me to road mangle her, and I did that for many years.

I would take a bullet for her, and there were times she had to ask me to back off. She took away my cattle prod early on, but I was always concerned that someone might hurt her in some way, and that would get me grumpy. One time in England, a guy came up to me and said, "I've got this girl and she's better than Emmylou. I want her to sing with Emmylou." I said, "Follow me," and took him to the dressing room area. And then I decked him. He fell through a swinging door, like in some western movie.

She loves what she's doing. She loves to sing, and she loves different kinds of music. She'll be on the bus, listening to Hungarian folk songs. She's very kind to up-and-coming artists, and she's a very, very good rhythm guitar player. Most of all, she was never afraid: She worked without a net.

When I had prostate cancer, she and Monty Hitchcock put together a benefit concert for me. When I had my motorcycle accident—I was 80, going sixty-five miles-per-hour on my motorcycle and then going sixty-five miles-per-hour not on my motorcycle—the first person I saw in the hospital was Emmylou, with a lemon ice box pie.

I love her. But I digest . . .

PHIL KAUFMAN
ROAD MANGLER DELUXE

SONGBIRD'S FLIGHT

BY PETER COOPER

Here is a story in which an eager, gifted, and floundering young artist finds her way to a place as one of American music's greatest and most impactful recording artists, collaborators, and community builders.

Through the decades, Emmylou Harris has inspired singers, players, and listeners to discover beauty and authenticity in music. She won a Grammy for her recording of a song called "The Connection," and a connection to Harris is a seal of credibility for other significant artists, who gravitate to her and to the people she has worked with.

Johnny Cash? Sang with Harris on "River of Jordan," and called her his favorite female vocalist.

Harris, 1976.
Photo: Dan Reeder

Miranda Lambert? Recorded the Harris standard "Easy From Now On," and gets goosebumps when people mention Harris album titles like *Red Dirt Girl* and *Wrecking Ball*.

Garth Brooks? His producer was Allen Reynolds, who co-produced Harris's luminous *Cowgirl's Prayer* and *Brand New Dance* albums and who wrote "Dreaming My Dreams," recorded by Harris.

Alison Krauss? Sang with Harris on the *O Brother, Where Art Thou?* soundtrack, and followed in Harris's footsteps by fronting blockbuster, bluegrass-based albums. And Krauss is in a band with Jerry Douglas, who was an integral player on Harris's *Roses in the Snow*.

The Louvin Brothers? Harris restored the brother duo's legacy by bringing their "If I Could Only Win Your Love" to country radio in the 1970s.

Keith Urban? Took "Making Memories of Us" to the top of the country charts. "Making Memories of Us" was written by Rodney Crowell, who got his start playing in Harris's Hot Band.

We can move beyond country music, play the same game, and easily find immediate connections with Bono, Sheryl Crow, Bob Dylan, Dan Fogelberg, Lowell George, Mark Knopfler, Little Richard, Paul McCartney, Keith Richards, Linda Ronstadt, Bruce Springsteen, Mavis Staples, Neil Young, and so many others.

Harris sometimes chalks all of this up to luck, but one of her baseball heroes — she's a big baseball fan — was a Dodgers executive named Branch Rickey, who integrated America's pastime in 1947 when he signed Jackie Robinson to a major league contract. Rickey used to say, "Luck is the residue of design."

Harris didn't design the precise course of her life, but she fashioned a musical approach, an intellectual curiosity, and an ethic of openness and generosity that assured a gargantuan realm of possibility and that enabled a delightful and fulfilling body of work.

She mastered the ability to derive lustrous results in times of turmoil. In those times, she built her solo career, she brought bluegrass music to country's mainstream, she helped save the Ryman Auditorium from destruction, she created a template for Americana music, and she wrote her truth.

In song, Harris once described this process as a "stumble into grace." It's also a beautiful arc, a songbird's flight through wondrous terrains.

Harris wore this Amy Michelson for Holly Harp shawl and gown at the 1999 Grammy Awards.

Opposite page: Harris, c.1975.
Photos: Dan Reeder

Harris, early 1950s

Bright Morning Stars

Born in Birmingham, Alabama, to Eugenia Murchison Harris and Walter "Bucky" Harris, Emmylou Harris was a military daughter whose Marine pilot father was a prisoner of war for nine months in Korea. He returned to the U.S., tortured but unbowed, and the family moved several times before settling in Woodbridge, Virginia, when Emmylou was ten. At fifteen, her grandfather bought her a Kay guitar for Christmas, and she began singing and playing folk music from Bob Dylan, Ian & Sylvia, Joan Baez, and others, as well as the country music favored by

Harris was six when she and her family reunited with her father, Walter "Bucky" Harris, following his release from a Chinese prison camp in 1953. From left: Mary Nell Murchison, Dewey Murchison Jr., Debbie Murchison, Eugenia Harris, Emmylou Harris, Walter Harris, Walter Harris Jr., Dewey Murchison Sr., Emma Lou Murchison, Mary Ann Murchison.

Military decorations awarded to Harris's father for service in World War II and the Korean War include the Legion of Merit and the Purple Heart.

her older brother, Walter Harris Jr. As a high school senior, she won the Miss Woodbridge beauty pageant, which allowed her to secure a scholarship to the University of North Carolina at Greensboro. There, she studied drama but discovered that her love for music trumped her interest in theater. In 1967, she dropped out of school and headed for New York City's Greenwich Village, to live at a YWCA and to sing.

Harris's first guitar, this Kay 1160 Deco Note was a Christmas present from her grandfather.

Emmylou Harris, formerly a drama major at UNC-G, has been making her way in the entertainment world since she left campus. She is presently appearing at the "Folk Ghetto" in Norfolk, Virginia, and at "The Upstairs" in Virginia Beach.

According to her former roommate, Sue Porto, Emmylou plans to enter the University of Boston in the fall as a drama student. Out of 368 applicants, Emmylou is one of 75 to be accepted to the prestigious drama school at Boston. Part of her reasons for leaving UNC-G was to earn the money necessary to attend Boston University.

Before Believing

Emmylou Harris played the Bitter End, Gerde's Folk City, and other venues in New York City, and she spent late nights at the Colonial Diner in Middletown, New York. "I remember sitting there—talking, getting excited about creating music, and hoping and praying that one day people would really pay attention to what you were trying to say," she told the Middletown *Times Herald Record*. In 1970, she recorded

Top left: Newspaper clipping, 1967.

Top right: Harris and John Starling, c. 1970.

From left: Harris; unidentified bass player; and guitarist Mike Williams, her partner in folk duo Emerald City, c. 1967.

her debut album, *Gliding Bird*, for Jubilee Records. "It showed my folk influences, and my voice was so young," she said. "The 'baby voice.'" The record was not a commercial success, and Harris moved to Nashville, waiting tables at the High Hat Lounge and hoping for a shot at a life in music. After six months, she and her young daughter retreated to her parents' home in Clarksville, Maryland, near Washington, D.C.

Left: When she was eighteen, in 1965, Harris wrote this letter to the editor of *Sing Out!*, a quarterly journal of folk music.

Harris's debut album, *Gliding Bird*, included her version of Bob Dylan's "I'll Be Your Baby Tonight," released as a single in 1970.

SingOut Vol 15 #4 Sept, 1965
P. 112

Dear Editor:

I have never voiced my opinions before (lazy, I guess) but perhaps now is just as good a day as any. All I want to say is that I don't always agree with your opinions, but you have the guts to stand up for them, which very few publications do.

Also, I would like to request an article on John Hammond, Jr.

Just one more thing. How can I go about getting honest criticism on my singing and playing style? I am not interested in becoming a professional, but I do enjoy performing and would appreciate honest help and advice from someone who knows.

Sincerely yours,

Emmy Lou Harris
Woodbridge, Va.

Troubles and Trials

In and around Washington, Emmylou Harris joined a community of musicians whose creativity and companionship reinvigorated a love of singing and playing that had flagged in the wake of her failed album *Gliding Bird*. During the day, she showed model homes in Columbia, Maryland. At night, she played small clubs and interacted with people including singer-songwriter Bill Danoff, John Starling of progressive bluegrass band the Seldom Scene, and Starling's wife, harmony vocalist Fayssoux Starling. All three would become key contributors in Harris's recording career. Harris was singing at Clyde's restaurant in

Georgetown, when three members of country-rock band the Flying Burrito Brothers—Chris Hillman, Rick Roberts, and Kenny Wertz—heard her and were impressed. Soon after, Hillman called his friend Gram Parsons, who was looking for a harmony singer. "I told Gram, 'You ought to look up this girl in Washington. You might have something in common,'" recalled Hillman, who was correct in his assessment.

Harris and Gram Parsons rehearsing with drummer N.D. Smart II and bass player Kyle Tullis, 1973.
Photos: © Kim Gottlieb-Walker, www.Lenswoman.com, all rights reserved.

Opposite page: Harris acquired this 1962 Gibson Country & Western model guitar early in her career.

I Saw the Light

In early 1972, Gram Parsons and wife Gretchen walked into Clyde's restaurant, where Emmylou Harris was playing to a nearly empty room. Between sets, Parsons and Harris sang a Hank Williams song, "I Saw the Light," amid basement beer kegs, finding a vocal blend that was striking and effortless. After the gig, they continued singing, at the home of musician Walter Egan. That autumn, Harris flew to Los Angeles to sing harmonies on Parsons's solo debut, *GP*.

Previously owned and used by **Gram Parsons**, this 1963 Gibson J-200N became Harris's main guitar for performing and recording.

Opposite page, from left: **Gram Parsons, drummer N.D. Smart II, Harris, and Kyle Tullis at Liberty Hall, Houston, Texas, February 1973.**
Photo: Doug Hanners - Austin Record Convention

Above: Gram Parsons and the Fallen Angels, 1973. Front row, from left:
Kyle Tullis, Harris, Jon Corneal, N.D. Smart II, Parsons, and Phil Kaufman. Back row,
from left: Gretchen Parsons (playing guitar), music writer Cameron Crowe, unidentified,
and *Music World* Magazine editor Jeff Walker.

RIght: Harris wore this Nudie's Rodeo Tailors shirt and skirt in performance
with Gram Parsons and during her solo career.

Opposite page: Phil Kaufman and Gram Parsons, 1973.

1963 Martin 00-21 and road case, owned and used by Gram Parsons.

Their partnership lasted less than two years, but was
highly impactful. For Harris, it was an immersion into the
blend of rock, soul, and traditional country that Parsons
called "Cosmic American Music." Parsons overdosed and
died in September 1973, at age twenty-six, but even now
he continues to inspire his duet partner. "I never realized
what kind of music was inside me until I met Gram," she
said. "Then I knew exactly what I wanted to do and where
I was going, but then he was gone."

Opposite page:
The Fallen Angels, 1973.
Standing from left:
Neil Flanz, Kyle Tullis,
Gram Parsons, Gerry Mule.
Kneeling:
N.D. Smart II, Harris.
Photo: Roy Carr

Left: Harris was Parsons's
duet partner on the
Fallen Angels' 1973 tour
that included shows at
Houston's Liberty Hall.

Below: Harris sang with
Parsons on his second
solo album, *Grievous
Angel*. At the 1973
recording sessions in
Hollywood, steel guitarist
Al Perkins used these
lead sheets for Parsons's
songs "$1000 Wedding"
and "Sleepless Nights."

Stumbling into Grace

Shaken by the death of her friend and mentor Gram Parsons, Emmylou Harris returned to the DC-area music scene, playing shows at Bethesda, Maryland's Red Fox Inn, and often attending late night jam sessions at the home of John and Fayssoux Starling. At the urging of Gram Parsons's manager, Eddie Tickner, music executive Mary Martin heard Harris at the Red Fox, signed her to Warner Bros., and teamed her with Brian Ahern, the brilliant Canadian producer. Ahern signed Nashville songwriter Rodney Crowell to a publishing contract and arranged for Crowell to attend one of the Starlings'

Rodney Crowell was using this 1971 Martin D-35 when he began working with Harris.

Opposite page: Harris at a recording session, early 1970s.

Harris, c. 1975.
Photo: Dan Reeder

Right: Hand-tooled leather guitar strap.

Opposite page: This one-of-a-kind shirt depicts the Enactron Truck, Brian Ahern's mobile studio.

Harris in Dallas, Texas, 1974. *Photo: Ron McKeown*

jam sessions. In Crowell, Harris found an artistic soulmate, an ideal singing partner, and a writer of captivating songs. In Ahern, she found an inventive producer who would help her make a mark on country music history. In 1974, Ahern, Harris, and Crowell headed to Los Angeles, and Ahern arranged for his forty-foot Enactron Truck recording studio-on-wheels to be driven to Los Angeles. Then they set about making Harris's major label debut.

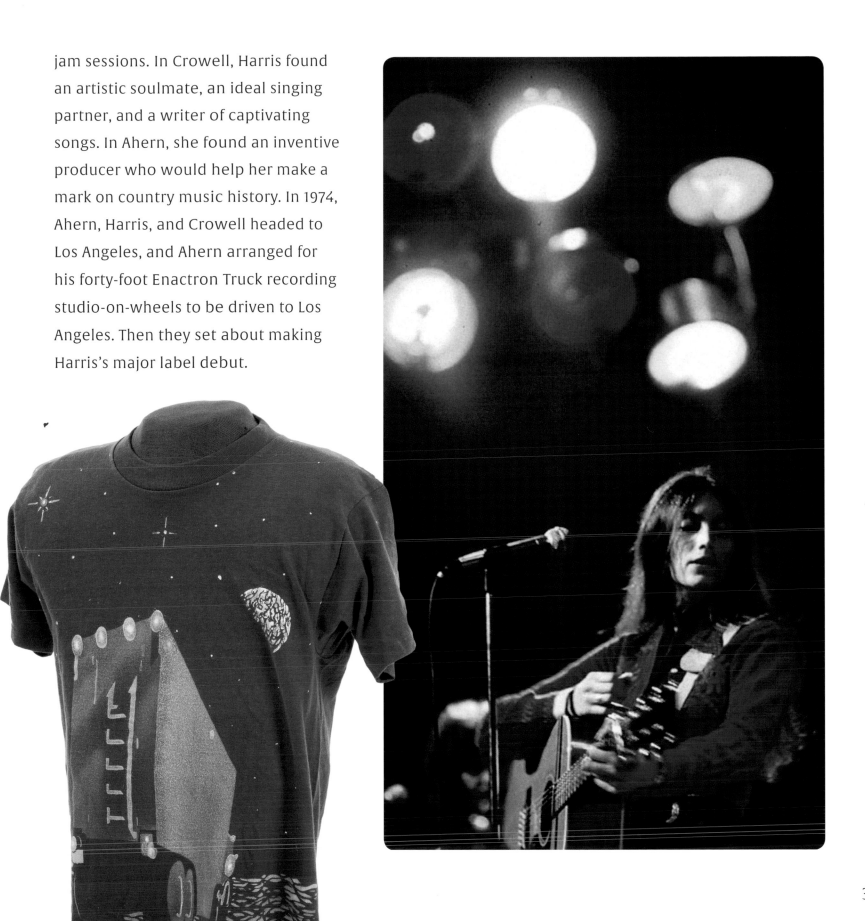

Above from left: Rodney Crowell, Harris, and Albert Lee, 1976.
Photo: Dan Reeder

Opposite page: Harris acquired this 1955 Gibson J-200 with custom black
finish in the 1970s. The rose inlay was added by luthier Danny Ferrington.

Pieces of the Sky

Brian Ahern parked his lead-lined Enactron Truck outside a rented ranch house on Lania Lane in Beverly Hills, and ran cables to microphones in various rooms of the house. He and Harris decided on a blend of musicians, some who had worked on Gram Parsons's albums, and others (Rodney Crowell, Fayssoux Starling) who were hand-picked to provide comfort and energy. Put off by the sterility of the Coldwater Canyon setting, Harris placed a Dolly Parton album cover on

Above: *The Washington Post*,
October 26, 1975

Right: Promotional poster, 1975

the mantle to, in Harris's words, "bless the proceedings." In February 1975, Warner Bros. released Harris's *Pieces of the Sky*. Crowell's "Bluebird Wine" opened the album, and the album title came from a line in Danny Flowers's ethereal "Before Believing." The album's emotional centerpiece was "Boulder to Birmingham," written by Harris with D.C.-area friend Bill Danoff in the despair that followed Gram Parsons's death. While initial single "Too Far Gone" failed to connect with country radio programmers, follow-up "If I Could Only Win Your Love"—sung with Herb Pedersen—reached #4 on *Billboard*'s country chart. For the first time, Harris was in the limelight.

Right: Harris wore this tunic with fringe and embroidery on the cover of her album *Elite Hotel*, released in 1975.

Above: Concert ticket for New York's Bottom Line, 1975.

EMMYLOU HARRIS
&
THE HOT BAND

FRAGILE

FRAGILE

The Hot Band, 1976. From left: Rodney Crowell, Emory Gordy Jr., Emmylou Harris, Hank DeVito, Albert Lee, Glen D. Hardin, John Ware, and Harris's daughter Hallie Slocum.
Photo: Dan Reeder

Guitar case for Rodney Crowell's 1971 Martin D-35.

Opposite page: Harris played this 1968 Fender Telecaster with custom paisley finish on her 1982 live album *Last Date*. The instrument was given to her by James Burton.

The Hot Band

Remembering some advice from Gram Parsons to "pay for the best" when choosing road musicians, Emmylou Harris made a crucial and ultimately fortuitous decision to bring studio aces James Burton, Glen D. Hardin, and Emory Gordy Jr. into her band. She added Rodney Crowell, John Ware, and Hank DeVito, securing a stack of aces that meant she would go deep into debt on tour, while enjoying one of the finest bands in country music. That band drew rave reviews in the summer of 1975, opening shows for Merle Haggard, James Taylor, and others. Its members also served as core musicians for a string of tremendous albums in the 1970s and early '80s. As band members moved on, they were replaced with players who

39

would go on to make grand marks in music: piano player (and, later, landmark producer) Tony Brown; steel guitarist Steve Fishell; fleet-fingered guitarist Albert Lee; bluegrass-reared Ricky Skaggs; and guitarist-vocalist Barry Tashian are among the many players who came through the group that Harris named "The Hot Band."

Below: Satin tour jacket worn by Tony Brown, the Hot Band's piano player on the 1978 tour promoting Harris's album *Quarter Moon in a Ten Cent Town*.

Right: Rodney Crowell, Harris, and James Burton, 1976. *Photo: Dan Reeder*

Bottom right: The Hot Band, 1978. From left: Ricky Skaggs, John Ware, Albert Lee, Harris, Glen D. Hardin, Emory Gordy Jr., Hank DeVito.

Clockwise, from top left: Harris and the Hot Band, 1976; James Burton; Burton and Hank DeVito in the studio; Rodney Crowell, Hank DeVito, Glen D. Hardin, Harris, John Ware, James Burton, and Emory Gordy Jr., early 1976; Crowell, Harris, Emory Gordy Jr., and Byron Berline, c. 1975.
Photos: Dan Reeder

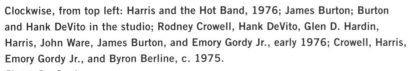

Left: Harris and the Hot Band opening for Elton John at Dodger Stadium, Los Angeles, October 25, 1975.
Above: Harris at the Universal Amphitheater, Los Angeles, July 1977.
Photos: Dan Reeder

Harmony Queen

Emmylou Harris has always been intrigued by what she calls "the third voice," meaning the unique tones achieved when two singers come together in harmony. That third voice is different with each pairing. By July 1975, Harris had sung famously with Gram Parsons, Herb Pedersen, and Rodney Crowell when she got a call to provide prominent harmony vocals throughout Bob Dylan's album *Desire*. Ultimately, she would do hundreds of sessions, leading her to a place among the most

distinctive and appreciated harmony singers in American music history. Her harmonies are notable not only for note choices and phrasing, but also for a dusky gravity peculiar to Harris's vocal blends. She has recorded with Dylan, Johnny Cash, Willie Nelson, Neil Young, Bruce Springsteen, Rosanne Cash, Dan Fogelberg, and many more.

Clockwise from top: Harris with Johnny Cash, 1981; Harris with Don Williams. Their duet on Townes Van Zandt's "If I Needed You" was a Top Five country hit in 1981; Ray Edwards, Tom T. Hall, and Harris on the syndicated TV series *Pop! Goes the Country*, 1980; Linda Ronstadt, Dolly Parton, and Emmylou Harris on *Dolly!*, Parton's syndicated TV show, 1976.

Opposite page: Harris provided harmony vocals on Bob Dylan's album *Desire* (1976). She received this commemorative platinum album for sales of more than one million copies.; Harris in the studio with Willie Nelson and producer Daniel Lanois, recording Nelson's album *Teatro*, 1998. *Photo: Danny Clinch*

EMMYLOU HARRIS - BLUE KENTUCKY GIRL

Blue Kentucky Girl

One of country music's leading ladies by the late 1970s, Emmylou Harris was stung by assertions of some critics that the albums she made with Brian Ahern (by then her husband), the Hot Band, and guests weren't truly country. At the same time, she was re-working the Hot Band's sound after the departure of Rodney Crowell, who left to pursue a solo career.

Harris asked Ricky Skaggs, a bluegrass-grounded singer and multi-instrumentalist, to replace Crowell, and Skaggs's entry rekindled Harris's love of deeply traditional music, instilled during her DC days. (She had met Skaggs at John and Fayssoux Starling's home in the early 1970s). Skaggs had a major impact on Harris's pure-country album *Blue Kentucky Girl*, released in May 1979. It was the antithesis of the pop replications that ruled country radio. The album and tour gave Skaggs his first international acclaim, and Harris scored a hit album, a Grammy, and her first top female vocalist prize from the Country Music Association.

Ricky Skaggs and Harris at the Grand Ole Opry, May 30, 1980.
Photo: Les Leverett / Image courtesy of Grand Ole Opry Archives.

Roses in the Snow

One of Harris's most significant albums is *Roses in the Snow*, from 1980, which brought unamplified instruments, bluegrass instrumentation, and shimmering harmonies to the forefront. Ricky Skaggs provided strong duets on the Louvin Brothers' "You're Learning" and gospel chestnut "The Darkest Hour Is Just Before Dawn." Acoustic guitar ace Tony Rice took several masterful solos, and the dobro of Jerry Douglas and the autoharp of Bryan Bowers sounded unlike anything else on country radio of the day. Though record executives worried that it would not sell well, *Roses in the Snow* was a rarity: a female-fronted, bluegrass-leaning album that found

Harris on the Dutch TV program *Top Pop*, 1981.

48

commercial success, setting the table for the new traditionalist movement of the early 1980s and for later triumphs by Alison Krauss and her band, Union Station. "It was a risky thing to do," Harris said. "Not just from the standpoint of my own constituency, but from the standpoint of real bluegrass people who might resent me doing it."

This photo by Olivier Ferrand was the cover art for Harris's album *Cimarron* (1981).

Right: Harris and Kitty Wells were presenters at the CMA Awards, 1981.
Photo: Ricky Rogers

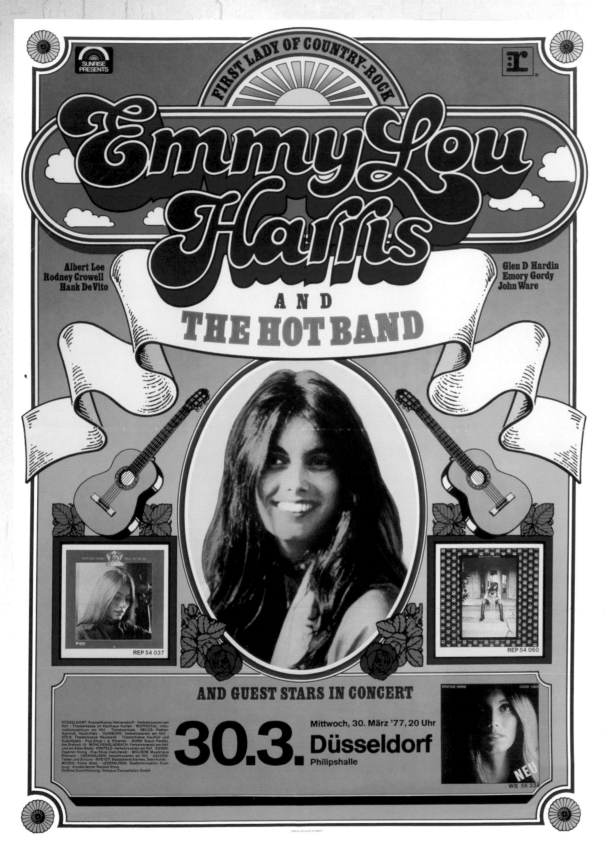

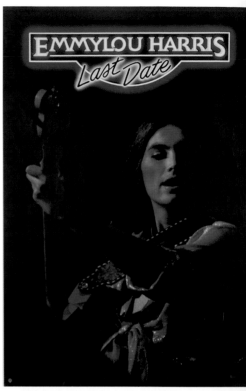

50

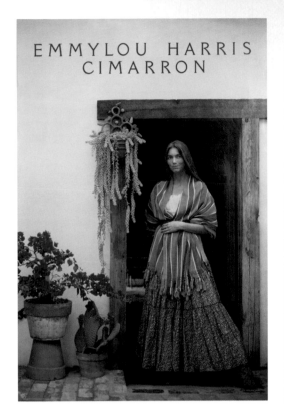

EMMYLOU HARRIS
CIMARRON

Emmylou Harris

The Ballad Of Sally Rose

EMMYLOU HARRIS

EVANGELINE

WARNER THEATRE MUSIC HALL

EARL SCRUGGS REVUE * EMMYLOU HARRIS * EMMYLOU HARRIS * EARL SCRUGGS REVUE

202-965-9650

SUNDAY, MARCH 28, 1976.....Shows: 7:30 & 10:30

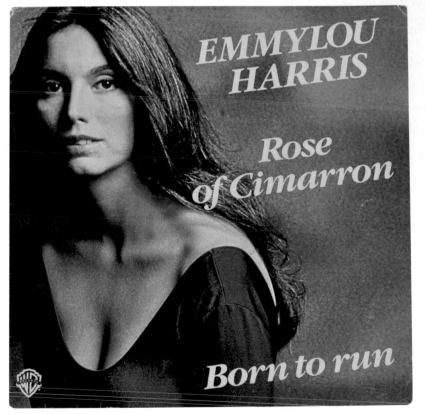

EMMYLOU HARRIS

Rose of Cimarron

Born to run

51

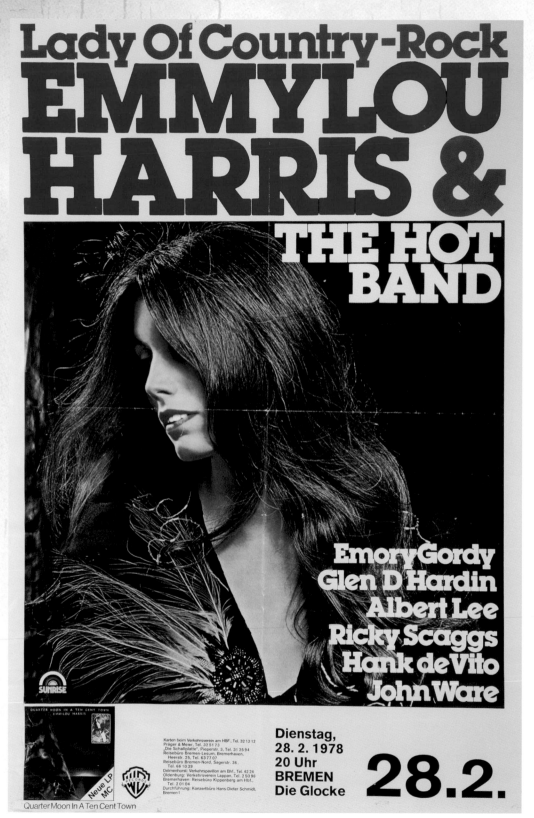

Ballad of Sally Rose

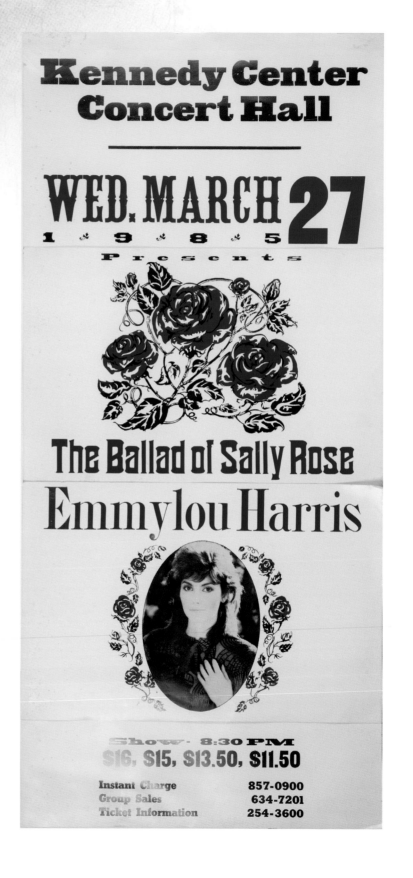

Kennedy Center Concert Hall

WED. MARCH 27
1 9 8 5

Presents

The Ballad of Sally Rose
Emmylou Harris

Show 8:30 PM
$16, $15, $13.50, $11.50

Instant Charge   857-0900
Group Sales   634-7201
Ticket Information   254-3600

After collaborating on more successful albums (*Cimarron*, *Last Date*, and *White Shoes*) and singles ("Born to Run" and the Don Williams duet "If I Needed You"), Emmylou Harris and Brian Ahern ended their marriage and temporarily halted their professional relationship. Harris moved to Nashville in the fall of 1983, and began working with acclaimed producer and songwriter Paul Kennerley. Together, she and Kennerley wrote *The Ballad of Sally Rose* (1985) a loosely autobiographical concept album that included melodic and poetic ruminations on Harris's relationship with Gram Parsons. "I've never been terrified of making an album, except for this one," she said. "I felt stripped bare." *The Ballad of Sally Rose* stands as an artistic turning point for Harris, as she flexed songwriting muscles to great effect and established herself in Nashville, where she has lived for thirty-five years.

Opposite page: Poster for a 1985 concert in Washington D.C.

Below: Handwritten lyrics by Paul Kennerley to "Diamond in My Crown" and "White Line." Co-written by Harris and Kennerley, both songs were included on *The Ballad of Sally Rose*.

Right: Harris, c. 1985.
Photo: Michel Pobeau

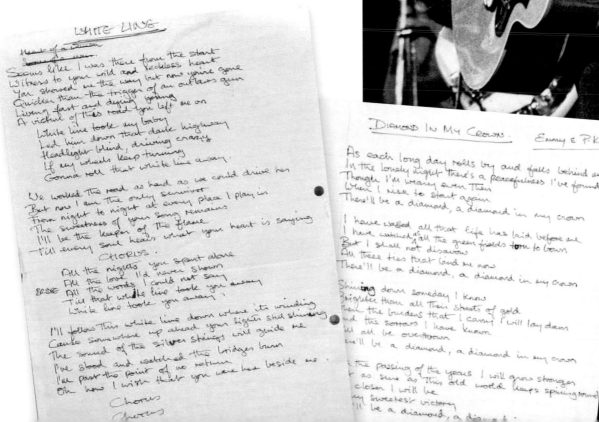

A Singular Trio

Steve Fishell played this Weissenborn Style One Hawaiian guitar on *Trio* and in performance. Made of koa wood, the instrument was built in the 1920s by luthier Hermann Weissenborn.

In January 1986, Emmylou Harris, Dolly Parton, and Linda Ronstadt began recording an album with George Massenburg producing and John Starling serving as musical director. "Our three voices became something completely different from what any of us do as individuals," Harris said. "It blew me away." Released in March 1987, and buoyed by instrumental contributions from Steve Fishell, Albert Lee, David Lindley, Mark O'Connor, and other masters, *Trio* topped *Billboard*'s country album chart, made its way into the Top Ten of *Billboard*'s all-genre album chart, and contained hit singles "Telling Me Lies," "To Know Him Is to Love Him," "Those Memories of You," and "Wildflowers." The album sold more than four million copies and won a country collaboration Grammy. A follow-up, 1999's *Trio II*, won another Grammy. "The Trio will always hold a special place in my musical life and in my heart," Harris said.

Above: Harris wore this Manuel jacket on the cover of *Trio* and in performance with Dolly Parton and Linda Ronstadt.

Top right: Promotional poster

Bottom right: Grammy for Best Country Performance by a Duo or Group with Vocal, 1987, presented to Harris for *Trio*.

At the Ryman

Having disbanded the Hot Band, Emmylou Harris formed an all-star acoustic group in the early 1990s. That group, the Nash Ramblers, included drummer Larry Atamanuik, multi-instrumentalists Sam Bush and Jon Randall Stewart, bass ace Roy Huskey Jr., and dobro player Al Perkins (who had played on Gram Parsons's albums). Harris had recently joined the Grand Ole Opry and was determined to record a live album at the rapidly decaying Ryman Auditorium, the Opy's former house, where no one was allowed to sit in or under the balcony, for fear of disaster. Recorded in April and May of 1991, *At the Ryman* featured classics from Boudleaux Bryant, Cowboy Jack Clement, and Bill Monroe, along with newer gems by Steve Earle, Nanci Griffith, and the songwriting team of Kieran Kane and Jamie O'Hara. The album and a television special revived interest in the Ryman and in Nashville's downtown, setting the table for a renaissance.

Travel itinerary for Emmylou Harris & the Nash Ramblers World Tour 91.

Below: Backstage pass, 1991.

Grammy for Best Country Performance by a Duo or Group with Vocal, 1992, for *At the Ryman*.

Wrecking Ball

By 1994, the writing was on the wall, and Emmylou Harris could read it. She had not had a Top Ten country single in six years, despite some inspired recordings (among them, 1993's *Cowgirl's Prayer*, produced by Richard Bennett and Allen Reynolds), and it was clear to her that her run as a radio hit-maker was over. Rather than reacting with crippling frustration, she determined that the situation afforded her the freedom to create music without concern for airplay or contemporary trends. She enlisted producer Daniel Lanois, known for his work with Bob Dylan, the Neville Brothers, U2, and others, and made an

Harris with Daniel Lanois, 1994.
Photo: Bob Lanois

album with a genre-leaping spirit that marked her as the godmother of what is now known as Americana music. Working at East Nashville's Woodland Studios and Kingsway Studio in New Orleans with collaborators including Steve Earle, Lucinda Williams, and Neil Young, Harris emerged with an expansive, Grammy-winning effort.

Silk dress with beaded embellishments worn by Harris when she won a Grammy for *Wrecking Ball*.

Below: Grammy for Best Contemporary Folk Album, 1995, for *Wrecking Ball*.

NATIONAL ACADEMY OF RECORDING ARTS & SCIENCES
EMMYLOU HARRIS
BEST CONTEMPORARY FOLK ALBUM – 1995
"WRECKING BALL"

Harris in New Orleans, 1994.
Photo: Bob Lanois

Opposite Page: Harris at
Wrecking Ball sessions
Photo: Bob Lanois

Floral-print dress Harris wore
while recording *Wrecking Ball*.

New Buddy, O Brother

Emmylou Harris continued her experimental ways at the turn of the century. She formed Spyboy, an esoteric touring ensemble that included drummer Brady Blade, bass man Daryl Johnson, and multi-instrumentalist Buddy Miller, who succeeded Rodney Crowell, Ricky Skaggs, and Barry Tashian in a line of vital and inventive right-hand men onstage. Miller would go on to great success as a songwriter, producer, and performer. Harris wrote eleven of twelve songs for *Red Dirt Girl*, an album that focused critical attention on her songwriting eloquence and won a Grammy for Best Contemporary Folk Album in 2001. Harris returned to the Grammy stage in 2002, joining the Fairfield Four, John Hartford, Alison Krauss, Ralph Stanley, Gillian Welch, the Whites, and others in receiving Album of the Year honors for the rootsy, multi-million-selling movie soundtrack *O Brother, Where Art Thou?*

From left: Patty Loveless, Ralph Stanley, and Harris on the *Down from the Mountain* tour, 2002.

Harris's Grammy for *O Brother, Where Art Thou?*

Opposite page: Spyboy, 1998. From left: Brady Blade, Harris, Daryl Johnson, and Buddy Miller.

Song Scavenger

Prior to 2000, and with the notable exception of *The Ballad of Sally Rose*, Emmylou Harris relied on other songwriters for the vast majority of her repertoire. She took an active approach to finding superior material, listening voraciously until she found songs that fit her unique sensibilities. She emerged as an early champion of numerous writers who have since become celebrated and oft-covered.

Those writers' names read like a who's who of respected country and Americana song-scribes: T Bone Burnett, Carlene Carter, Marshall Chapman, Rodney Crowell, Guy and Susanna Clark, Danny Flowers, Mark Germino, Patty Griffin, Nanci Griffith, Butch Hancock, Kieran Kane, Kate and Anna McGarrigle, Buddy and Julie Miller, David Olney, Townes Van Zandt, Gillian Welch, Jesse Winchester, and many others saw their songs grow wings because of Harris's curatorial care and musical attention.

Opposte page: from left: Guy Clark, Harris, and Susanna Clark at the Banjo, Fiddle and Guitar Festival, California State University, Long Beach, California, April 1976.
Photo: Dan Reeder

Above top, from left: David Rawlings, Harris, and Gillian Welch at Newport Folk Festival, 2001.

Above: Buddy Miller and Harris at Miller's Artist-in-Residence performance, Country Music Hall of Fame and Museum, August 2010.
Photo: Donn Jones

Cup of Kindness

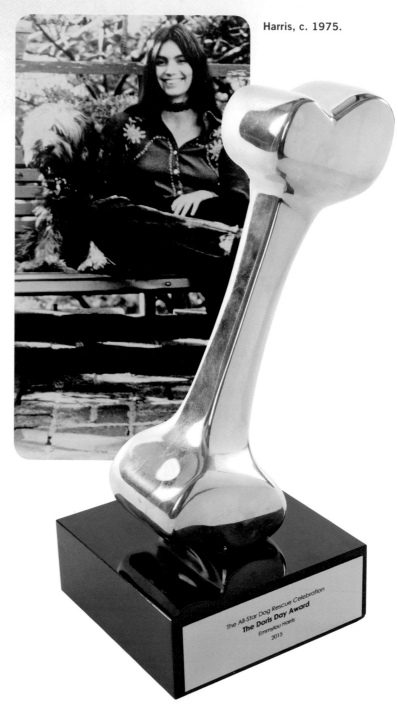

Harris, c. 1975.

In her more than thirty-five years in Nashville, Emmylou Harris has given her time and talent to many worthy endeavors. She served as president of the Country Music Foundation, aiding the mission of the Country Music Hall of Fame and Museum, and she regularly performs at the museum's All for the Hall fundraising concerts (sharing a stage with Vince Gill, Maren Morris, Paul Simon, Taylor Swift, and others). She supports landmine eradication efforts, performing with Mary Chapin Carpenter, Steve Earle, Nanci Griffith, Buddy Miller, and others, to raise funds and awareness. And she devotes personal time to Bonaparte's Retreat, overseeing the housing, training, and relocation of dogs that are in imminent danger of euthanization. Bonaparte's Retreat is named after her pet poodle-mix, Bonaparte, who toured with her for many years and is buried in her Nashville backyard. In Bonaparte's memory, and through Harris's vigilance, hundreds of dogs live long, love-filled lives.

To honor her work with Bonaparte's Retreat, Harris received the inaugural Doris Day Award at the All-Star Dog Rescue Celebration in Santa Monica, California, in 2015. The non-profit Doris Day Animal Foundation was founded by the Hollywood actress in 1978.

Opposite page: Emmylou Harris and her dogs. May 2000.
Photo: ©Michael Wilson

Elvis Costello, Gillian Welch, Harris, Viktor Krauss, and David Rawlings at the Grand Ole Opry, February 8, 2006.
Photo: Chris Hollo / Image courtesy of the Grand Ole Opry Archives.

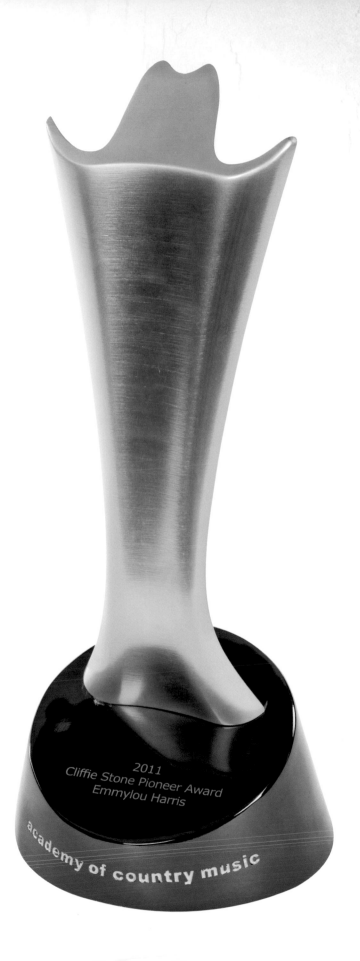

An Ongoing Flight

Emmylou Harris's new-century triumphs include the solo albums *Red Dirt Girl*, *Stumble Into Grace*, *All I Intended to Be* (produced by Brian Ahern, who helped guide her early career), and *Hard Bargain*, as well as pleasing collaborations with Mark Knopfler and her old Hot Band mate Rodney Crowell. She remains a creative force, collecting awards for lifetime achievement even as she extends that lifetime and confounds expectations. She is writing a memoir by hand,

Cliffie Stone Pioneer Award presented to Harris by the Academy of Country Music in 2011.

Above: Patsy Montana Entertainer Award presented to Harris by the National Cowgirl Hall of Fame in 1996, for her work in advancing the tradition of the cowgirl in her music.

Left: Harris wore this Manuel dress when she sang harmonies and played rhythm guitar with Neil Young at Nashville's Ryman Auditorium, August 18-19, 2005. The concerts were filmed and released as *Neil Young: Heart of Gold*, a documentary by Jonathan Demme.

setting down the story of her life even as she extends that story with every new song and recording. Friend and collaborator Linda Ronstadt calls Harris "uncompromising and tireless . . . She's got the profound respect of the entire musical community. There isn't anybody who's more revered."

Above: Grammy Lifetime Achievement Award, presented to Harris in 2018.

Right: Harris wore this custom-made Johnny Was embroidered dress and hooded jacket at the 2018 Grammys.

SUGGESTED LISTENING

At the Ryman, 1992. Warner Bros.

Recorded at Nashville's Ryman Auditorium, which was in terrible disrepair, this live gem features songs written by Steve Earle, Stephen Foster, Bill Monroe, Hank Williams, and others. For *At the Ryman*, Harris introduced her new band, the Nash Ramblers, including mandolin and fiddle king Sam Bush, extraordinary bass player Roy Huskey Jr., slide guitar great Al Perkins, and young multi-instrumentalist Jon Randall Stewart.

The Ballad of Sally Rose, 1985. Warner Bros.

Written with producer and songwriting force Paul Kennerley, *The Ballad of Sally Rose* is a fictional account of Harris's relationship with Gram Parsons. "Diamond in My Crown" was later recorded by Patty Loveless.

Old Yellow Moon (with Rodney Crowell), 2013. Nonesuch.

Reunited with friend and Hot Band member Rodney Crowell and with producer Brian Ahern, *Old Yellow Moon* contains Allen Reynolds's "Dreaming My Dreams" and a reprise of Crowell's "Bluebird Wine," which was the first track on Harris's debut album, *Pieces of the Sky*.

Pieces of the Sky, 1975. Warner Bros.

Harris's major-label debut, this contains the beautiful rumination "Boulder to Birmingham," written in the wake of Gram Parsons's death.

Quarter Moon in a Ten Cent Town, 1978. Warner Bros.

This one kicks off with "Easy From Now On," written by Carlene Carter and Susanna Clark, and includes songs from Rodney Crowell, Delbert McClinton, and Utah Phillips, with guest vocals from Willie Nelson and Fayssoux Starling.

Red Dirt Girl, 2000. Nonesuch.

Harris wrote or co-wrote eleven of twelve tracks in a return to top songwriting form. "Bang the Drum Slowly," written with Guy Clark, is an elegy for her father, a prisoner of war in Korea, while "Red Dirt Girl" is a masterpiece of narrative songwriting.

Roses in the Snow, 1980. Warner Bros.

Acoustic giants Jerry Douglas, Ricky Skaggs, and Tony Rice are at the forefront of an album that blends new-school virtuosity and mountain charm. The Harris and Skaggs duet on "Darkest Hour Is Just Before Dawn" is a study in singing and musicality, buoyed by producer Brian Ahern's mind-blowing modulations and transitions.

Songbird: Rare Tracks & Forgotten Gems, 2007. Rhino/Warner Bros.

This boxed set includes four CDs, a DVD, extensive liner notes, Harris's track-by-track commentary, and numerous songs that were unheard until its release. Highlights include very early gems from the Trio and a stunning take on Townes Van Zandt's "Snowin' on Raton."

Trio (Dolly Parton, Linda Ronstadt and Emmylou Harris), 1986. Warner Bros.

A richly rewarding collaboration between three spectacular singers, *Trio* contains four hit country singles, topped *Billboard*'s country album chart, and won a Grammy.

Wrecking Ball, 1995. Elektra.

On a short-list of albums that anticipated the new century's Americana music designation, *Wrecking Ball* is expansive and eclectic, with songs from Bob Dylan, Julie Miller, David Olney, Gillian Welch, Neil Young, and producer Daniel Lanois.

Memorable Emmylou Harris performances on other artists' recordings:

Solomon Burke. "We're Gonna Hold On," 2016.
Soul master Solomon Burke recorded this George Jones and Tammy Wynette classic with Harris. "I call her my queen," Burke said, introducing Harris at Nashville's Belcourt Theater, a one-time home of the Grand Ole Opry. "One of the greatest singers I've ever known."

Desert Rose Band. "The Price I Pay," 1991.
Here, Harris sings with DRB lead singer Chris Hillman, who helped introduce her to Gram Parsons. John Jorgenson's rocket-fueled guitar solo has influenced six-stringers including Brad Paisley.

Bob Dylan. "One More Cup of Coffee," 1976.
Dylan's gypsy tale, with prominent Harris harmonies, is part of his album *Desire*, recorded in 1975.

Patty Griffin. "Trapeze," 2007.
Splendid Griffin-penned song, uplifted by Harris's backing vocals.

Jim Lauderdale. "The King of Broken Hearts," 1991.
Lauderdale wrote this about two of his heroes — George Jones and Gram Parsons — and Harris supplies harmonies on the song, later recorded by George Strait and Lee Ann Womack.

Willie Nelson. "Somebody Pick Up My Pieces," 1998.
Harris provided harmonies for much of Nelson's *Teatro*, including this slow and devastating Nelson-written song.

Gram Parsons. "Love Hurts," 1974.
This Boudleaux Bryant-written ballad was the ideal vehicle to showcase a remarkable vocal blend.

The War and Treaty.
"Here Is Where the Lovin' Is At," 2018.
The duo of Michael and Tanya Trotter feature Harris on this grammatically incorrect but emotionally powerful recording.

Lucinda Williams. "Greenville," 1998.
From Williams's Grammy-winning breakthrough album, *Car Wheels on a Gravel Road*, "Greenville" is a ballad of busted love.

On the Cover

Tom Wilkes, who photographed Emmylou Harris for the 1975 album package of *Pieces of the Sky*, created some of rock's seminal album covers as an art director, designer, and photographer. One of the photographs (above, right) from the Harris photo shoot is the basis for the museum exhibition's look and this book's cover design. He was the Monterey International Pop Festival's first art director, and notably went on to produce classic album art for the Rolling Stones' *Beggars Banquet*, Janis Joplin's *Pearl*, George Harrison's *All Things Must Pass*, and Neil Young's *Harvest*, among others. He earned a Grammy in 1973 for his design of the album package for *Tommy*, by the London Symphony Orchestra and Chamber Choir. He died in 2009.

Wilkes's photograph appears with the permission of his daughter, Katherine Wilkes Harvill.

CIRCLE GUARD

The Country Music Hall of Fame and Museum Circle Guard unites and celebrates individuals who have given their time, talent, and treasure to safeguard the integrity of country music and make it accessible to a global audience through the Museum. The Circle Guard designation ranks as the grandest distinction afforded to those whose unwavering commitment to the Museum protects the legacies of the members of the Country Music Hall of Fame, and, by extension, the time-honored achievements of all who are part of the country music story.

2018 INAUGURAL CLASS

Steve Turner, Founder

Kyle Young, Commander General

David Conrad

J. William Denny

Mary Ann McCready

Seab Tuck

Harris and her daughter Hallie Slocum, Coldwater Canyon, California, 1976.
Photo: Michael Dobo / Dobophoto.com